FORENSIC DATA COLLECTIONS 2.0

The Guide for Defensible & Efficient Processes

Robert B. Fried

Wingspan Press

This publication is designed to provide accurate and authoritative information in regard to the subject matter covered. It is sold with the understanding that the publisher is not engaged in rendering legal, accounting, or other professional service. If legal advice or other expert assistance is required, the services of a competent professional should be sought.

Published in the United States and the United Kingdom
by WingSpan Press, Livermore, CA

The WingSpan name, logo and colophon are the trademarks
of WingSpan Publishing.

Publisher's Cataloging-in-Publication data
Names: Fried, Robert B., author.
Title: Forensic data collections 2.0 : the guide for defensible
& efficient processes / Robert B. Fried.
Description: Includes index. | Livermore, CA: Wingspan Press, 2021.
Identifiers: LCCN: 2021922575 | ISBN: 978-1-63683-018-6 (pbk.) |
978-1-63683-500-6 (hardcover)
Subjects: LCSH Forensic sciences--United States--Handbooks,
manuals, etc. | Evidence, Criminal--United States--Handbooks,
manuals, etc. | BISAC LAW / Forensic Science
Classification: LCC HV8073 .F5835 F75 2021 | DDC 363.25--dc23

First edition 2022

Printed in the United States of America

www.wingspanpress.com

Library of Congress Control Number: 2021922575

1 2 3 4 5 6 7 8 9 10

To Janet Nickel-Evola and Dr. Thomas A. Johnson, two wonderful educators who sparked my interest in forensic science and computer forensics, respectfully. Thank you for setting me forward on a path that has allowed me to discover my passion and do what I love each day.

Contents

Foreword

I have devoted my life's work to the field of Forensic Science and Investigation. During my 60 years in the field, there have been remarkable advances in Investigative Technology and Forensic Science as it relates to criminal and civil investigations. However, not all investigations have an abundance of physical evidence available, such as DNA, fingerprints, firearms, hairs, and fibers. Today, investigations depend on the collection and analysis of electronic evidence.

As Emeritus Professor and Founder of the Henry C. Lee Institute of Forensic Science at the University of New Haven (UNH), I had the opportunity to meet and educate the next generation of forensic scientists. I met Robert B. Fried while he was studying forensic science at UNH and taking courses in computer forensic investigation; twenty years later, he has become a thought leader in the field of digital forensics.

In *Forensic Data Collections 2.0*, Robert applies his academic knowledge - and his many years of professional experience - to share his masterful knowledge and provide valuable guidance relating to the identification, preservation, and collection of electronic evidence. Robert has spent most of his career sharpening his skills in digital forensics and educating law enforcement personnel, clients, colleagues, and students. His perseverance in compiling the content for *Forensic Data Collections 2.0* and his commitment to contributing important information to the field is apparent in the materials he authors and presents.

I trust that the knowledge Robert shares relating to electronic evidence will help us navigate the landscape of evolving evidence encountered today and provide a foundation to address newer types of evidence that will inevitably be on the horizon for the next generation.

Dr. Henry C. Lee
Vice President / Professor Emeritus, University of New Haven
Director, Forensic Research & Training Center
Founder, Henry Lee Institute of Forensic Science
Commissioner (Ret), Connecticut State Police / Dept of Public Safety
Director / Chief Criminalist (Ret), State Forensic Science Laboratory

September 2021

Preface

The field of digital forensics is continuously evolving. As I began my career as a forensics practitioner, the data sources of interest were primarily computers and mailboxes stored on an on-premises email server, and network files and folders stored on an on-premises file server. Now, there are many more classes of data sources to take into consideration and data can exist beyond our four walls. It is important to address and handle data that is potentially relevant to an investigation or litigation in a defensible and efficient manner, so that it may be admissible in a court of law, if necessary. With over twenty years of professional experience, as an instructor to law enforcement, and as a consultant to global corporations and law firms, I am pleased to share my knowledge and experience. The primary focus of *Forensic Data Collections 2.0* is to provide key information related to the identification, preservation, and collection of the most common data sources encountered today.

Robert B. Fried
October 2021

Acknowledgements

It would be difficult for me to list all the individuals who have been a positive influence on my life and career. I have kept in touch with many friends and colleagues throughout the years. I feel a sense of pride to have crossed paths with each of them. Thank you all.

A special thanks to my family who believed in my interest of the forensic sciences and supported me in various capacities as I progressed from academia to professional life. A special thank you to my parents, Alex and Penina and my siblings Brian and Jennifer.

My grandparents, Madga and Moshe Herskowitz and Rifka and Israel Fried have been a major influence throughout my life. I remember each of them daily with an immense amount of respect and pride, as they rebuilt their lives from ashes after surviving the horrors of the Holocaust.

Of course, I could not do what I do each day without the love and support of my wife, Rachael, a physician assistant, our son, Aaron, and daughter, Madeline. Thank you for bringing me a profound sense of purpose, pride, and joy. I love you all.

Introduction

In today's world we must be prepared for almost anything. It has been increasingly important to think on our feet and frequently compile customized workflows and solutions to meet our client's needs. The COVID-19 pandemic, the introduction of Bring Your Own Device (BYOD) policies, data privacy laws, and a heightened awareness and concern regarding data security has impacted how we go about addressing electronic evidence.

The reader will soon learn that the way data is collected for an investigation may be different than for an eDiscovery matter. It will also become apparent quickly that although many forensic tools and workflows have been developed over the years, there may not always be a solution readily available for a given scenario. When this happens, which will inevitably be the case, it may be necessary to be innovative, and ultimately, whatever workflow will be compiled and utilized must be validated on test data before it is implemented.

The content within, is primarily focused on matters and electronic evidence originating in the United States of America. There are fundamental concepts that are shared throughout; they all have the same objective — to approach the scenario that is encountered in the most defensible and efficient manner, documenting any actions performed throughout the process. It is not always possible to predict the outcome of a matter, but we must be forward thinking and thorough in all we do. This is important, not only for the short term to reflect on what occurred recently, but also for reference in the future, as many matters extend over years.

Most importantly, this publication serves as a guide with the intent of providing authoritative information about the dynamic field of digital forensics. It is vital to vet the information individually, and when required, seek the services of an expert or legal professional.

Electronically Stored Information (ESI)

ESI has evolved over the years. There has been a shift in both its definition and application in litigation matters. In the past, parties dealt primarily with hard-copy documents. I recall hearing stories from my colleagues about the days they spent sifting through banker boxes of documents to identify and subsequently organize the documents for scanning and eventual production. Nowadays, many types of data sources exist due to the tremendous advancements in technology. As a result, it has become necessary for the courts and legal professionals to make amendments. Although there have been enhancements to rules and standards, many of the underlying stages of the process specifically related to the identification, preservation and collection still apply. ESI, as we know it today, is defined as "information created, manipulated, communicated, stored and best utilized in digital form."

By its nature, ESI is fragile and therefore it must be handled with care. ESI may be invisible to the naked eye. Although we may not be able to see it, our actions can impact its integrity. It is important to follow guidelines and protocols that address the proper identification, preservation, and collection so that the source evidence remains unchanged. Additionally, time and environmental factors can impact ESI, which can have an impact on the accessibility of the data.

Electronic evidence is different than physical evidence. With electronic evidence, a forensic investigator can generate a snapshot in time of the data stored on an electronic device, such as: hard drives, thumb drives, mobile devices, and computers. There is no degradation of the source data throughout the identification, preservation, and collection stages. The same cannot be said in general for physical evidence, as a forensic investigator will likely need to perform testing on a sample of the source object. Types of physical evidence includes blood, drugs, guns, and fibers.

In the field of electronic discovery (e-discovery), many legal professionals utilize the Electronic Discovery Reference Model (EDRM) when addressing ESI, as it defines the various processes involved in its initial identification through its presentation. In fact, we have been discussing the first three stages, Identification, Preservation and Collection! The web site, edrm.net, is an excellent resource and provides the various definitions for the stages of the EDRM. During the Identification stage, potential sources of ESI are located and steps are taken to determine its scope, breadth and depth. The Preservation stage ensures that ESI is protected against alteration or destruction. The Collection stage involves the gathering of ESI for future use in the e-discovery process, specifically during the Processing, Review, Analysis, Production or Presentation stages. We will continue to focus on the first three stages, but when thinking about the EDRM it is important to realize that these stages may not always be followed in a particular order. They may not always be completed, and it is possible for stages to be repeated or refined.

Within each of the three stages, there are important topics and issues to take into consideration. For example, in the Identification stage, one should be aware of any court orders, protocols, or documentation that may be available for reference. Additionally, it is important to identify Key Individuals who may play a critical role in the matter. When dealing with matters involving a business, one should be aware of corporate documents or policies that may be in place. With the documentation and Key Individuals identified, one must begin to think about the various data sources that may be relevant. Be aware that just because something exists in a policy, it does not mean that there will be no deviations. When considering the Preservation stage, the question "to delete or not delete" will likely come up. It is critical during this stage to define, modify or suspend any data retention policies to protect the integrity of potentially relevant data and avoid the issue of spoilation. Finally, the Collection stage has several key considerations, including establishing chain of custody, and documenting information about the electronic devices containing ESI, and any processes performed. We will discuss each stage in more depth.

4

How Electronic Data is Stored

During the Identification stage, reference documentation such as a court order or protocol may be particularly useful, if available. These documents may provide background information to a matter, including party names, venue, subjects / issues related to the matter, types of data that may be relevant (documents and communication), relevant time periods, search terms / keywords, production formats, and deadlines. It is important to remember that things can always change, during a matter; therefore, utilize a strategy to identify potentially relevant ESI.

There are Key Individuals who are critical to confer with during the Identification Stage. Members of the Internal Legal Team and the Outside Counsel that they may engage are important. They assist in facilitating the overall strategy for a matter and any communication between the relevant parties. Data Custodians are those individuals who have control or access to information, ESI, or hard-copy documents that may be relevant to a matter. Business Stakeholders may also play an important role, as they have a vested interest in the business that may be involved in a matter. Last but certainly not least, members of the Information Technology (IT) Team or Designated Administrators are critical, as they will provide information about the internal and external corporate systems and resources that are available within an organization.

Protocols, policies, and other corporate documentation, provided by Key Individuals, may be useful, if available. For example, data storage and access policies can provide insight as to where potentially relevant data resides within a corporate network. There are different categories of data sources but at a very high level, they include local devices, network-based devices / data, backups and archive solutions, cloud-based services, and "other" data sources, including instant messaging and voicemail platforms.

Local devices: Includes corporate or personal, current, or previously used computers, mobile devices, external devices / media.

Network-based devices / data: Includes network email (located on / off premises), network file shares, databases.

<u>Backup and archive solutions</u>: Includes legacy systems and media.

<u>Cloud-based services</u>: Includes email, collaboration, computing, productivity, and storage solutions / services.

Something that is important to keep in mind, however, is that people don't always follow protocols or policies. More specifically, where people store data may deviate from where they are supposed to store data.

Preserving & Collecting Electronic Data

Again, the stage of Preservation involves the steps taken to ensure that ESI is protected against alteration or destruction. It is important to consider the potentially relevant data at issue and factors such as whether a business is involved. More specifically, identify and evaluate the risks involved when deciding whether data should or should not be deleted. Always keep in mind that the processes utilized should be defensible and efficient. They should not be overly burdensome and ensure that business continuity is not severely impacted.

Litigation matters can go on for an extended period, and preservation efforts must remain in effect until the matter is formally settled. It is important for the Internal Legal Team / Outside Counsel to work closely with the other Key Individuals to implement and enforce a legal hold, including defining or modifying data retention policies for persistent data, and suspending auto-deletion processes / recycling of backup media. It is recommended that periodic reminders be sent to the Key Individuals to ensure their compliance.

Documentation is one of the most important aspects of the Collection stage. A Chain of Custody Form is a document that records the transfer of possession of a device or storage media that contains potentially relevant ESI; it must be maintained throughout the life cycle of a matter. Although Chain of Custody Forms can take on different formats, the following fields should be listed:

- Matter Name
- Evidence Number Assigned
- Description of Device / Media
- Date and Time of Transfer (for each transfer that takes place)

- The Parties Involved (including printed names and signatures)

- The Purpose of the Transfer

As mentioned previously, ESI is fragile and can be easily destroyed. How electronic devices and media are stored is important, especially when there may be a gap in time between next steps. Devices and media should be placed in a secure location and the individual who has custody and control should ensure that optimal conditions exist, and proper precautions are taken to preserve ESI.

Photography and recording devices are useful in documenting the source device / media; specifically, they can be utilized to document the power state, condition, and any unique identifiers. For example, they can document if a source device / media is powered on or off, if it is in good physical condition and the make, model, serial number that may be visible on a physical label.

When considering how ESI can be collected, there are multiple options that may be available. One must decide whether a forensic image or a targeted collection is required. In any case, a data collection specialist will utilize specialized, forensic hardware and software to perform the data collection. These tools ensure that the integrity of the potentially relevant ESI is maintained, including any associated metadata (data about data). Metadata is of particular importance, and there are two types: internal (located within a file) and external (located outside a file).

A forensic image is a bit-by-bit copy of a device, and it gets all. Sometimes, a forensic image is referred to as a "bitstream" image or a "mirror" image. Generating a forensic image can be time consuming, as it includes files, the unpartitioned areas of storage media, the Unallocated Space of a storage volume, File Slack, and Partition Slack. It is important to dive into each of these a bit. Regarding files, those in an active and deleted state along with their associated metadata are included. When discussing the unpartitioned areas of storage media, this refers to areas that are not yet formatted with a file system. The Unallocated Space of a storage volume refers to the area of a file system that is available to store data. Unallocated Space is an area that a forensic investigator focuses on for the potential recovery of deleted data. File Slack refers to the area between the end of a file and the end of the last cluster (the smallest single unit of space on a storage volume) allocated to the file. The area known as Partition Slack refers to the area between the end of a file system and the end of the partition where the file system resides. Once the forensic image is generated, a forensic investigator can utilize forensic tools that allow for the analysis of each of these.

A targeted collection refers to the forensic preservation or file copy of specific files or folders. Targeted collections are typically faster than forensic images; they include only active files and not File Slack. There are many different tools and processes that are available to generate a targeted collection. The data collection specialist uses those that will be the most defensible and efficient, where the integrity of the source data (including its content and associated metadata) will be maintained.

The integrity of the forensic image or targeted collection is verified utilizing a hash algorithm; a unique value that is generated based on the contents of a data set. These hash values are often referred to as "digital fingerprints." Common hash algorithms used by the forensic community include Message Digest 5 (MD5), Secure Hash Algorithm 1 (SHA-1), and Secure Hash Algorithm 2 (SHA-2).

A MD5 hash consists of a 128-bit value and is 32 hexadecimal digits in length.

A SHA-1 hash consists of a 160-bit value and is 40 hexadecimal digits in length.

A SHA-2 hash consists of a 256-bit value and is 64 hexadecimal digits in length.

As mentioned previously, documentation is a key aspect of the Collection stage. The forensic tools that are utilized will very often generate log files. These files are typically autogenerated and document the processes performed.

Another form of documentation that is utilized during the Collection stage is a Forensic Acquisition Form. A data collection specialist will complete a new form for each data collection performed, to record information about the specific data source and process undertaken, including what was collected, when and by whom, along with any related notes. The following fields are often included on a Forensic Acquisition Form:

- Matter Name / Number
- Name of Data Custodian
- Date / Time of Collection
- Location of Collection
- Source Device / Media / Account Type
- Make / Model / Serial Number / Storage Capacity of the Source and Target Device / Media
- Name of Data Collection Specialist
- Name of Forensic Tool(s) utilized (including version) or methodologies utilized
- Encryption Solution (and version) Identified
- Type of Data Collection (Forensic image / Targeted collection)
- Evidence Name / Number
- Size of Collected Data
- Notes (including: Device Condition / Power State)

To keep track of what data was collected, a data collection specialist will actively maintain a Data Collection Log. A Data Collection Log should include the following fields:

- Matter Name / Number
- Name of Data Custodian (and priority level)
- Date / Time of Collection
- Location of Collection
- Source Device / Media / Account Type
- Make / Model / Serial Number / Storage Capacity of the Source and Target Device / Media
- Name of Data Collection Specialist
- Name of Forensic Tool(s) utilized (including version) or methodologies utilized

- Type of Data Collection (Forensic image / Targeted collection)
- Evidence Name / Number
- Size of Collected Data
- Notes

Understanding the difference between a forensic image and targeted collection is important; not just from a technical standpoint, but in terms of what is best for the matter. To make an informed decision, answer the following questions:

- Is this an eDiscovery matter or a forensic investigation?
- What data will be available?
- Is all potentially relevant ESI identified?
- What if there is a change in scope for the matter?

When dealing with a forensic investigation, a forensic image is recommended, so you have access to all. Recall the differences between a forensic image and targeted collection and consider what is included and excluded. Keep in mind that the Key Individuals may have sensitives that may need to be taken into consideration. It is important to ensure that all relevant data sources have been identified; for example, the Key Individuals may not recall the location of all files or folders. Remember that the scope of a matter may change. One must consider the following if a re-collection of data or another round of data collections is necessary: will the Key Individuals be available to provide access to the data, will the data still be available, and from a budgeting and resourcing standpoint, what additional costs and time would be involved?

Computers

There are various types of computers and configurations. We will focus on the most common, a desktop and a laptop. A desktop is meant to be stationary, whereas a laptop allows for mobility. It is possible for computers to be corporate-issued or personally owned.

Over the years, there have been enhancements to storage media. Where previously, hard disk drives (HDD) were primarily encountered, it is now common for computers to contain solid-state drives (SSD). Whereas HDD are storage devices with rotating platters, SSD are storage devices which utilize semiconductors. Storage capacities can range from gigabytes (GB) to terabytes (TB). It is important to know that depending on its configuration, some storage media may be removable, while others may be integrated. Although more technical in nature, it is good to be familiar with storage media interfaces, including Serial ATA (SATA), Mini-Serial ATA (mSATA), and Integrated Drive Electronics (IDE).

The type of computer that one uses may be influenced by several factors, including location, role, or personal preference. For example, a corporation may decide to issue a specific make and model desktop for all employees who work on-site at an office; the corporation may decide to issue a laptop to members of the sales team who work remotely. Additionally, there may be a need for an employee to have multiple computers. For example, the CEO of a corporation with multiple offices may travel with a laptop but may also have a desktop computer at each office location.

Identifying Relevant Data

It is important to identify if the computer is in scope; in other words, is potentially relevant data stored on the device? To understand what devices may be in use and if they are relevant, the following questions can be of asked of a Key Individual:

- What is the make / model of the computer?
- When was the computer issued?
- Was the computer in use during the relevant period?
- Was the computer new or repurposed?
- Was the computer issued as part of a technology refresh?
  - If yes, was data migrated over from a previously used computer?
  - If no, is the previously used computer or its data accessible?
- Have any issues with the computer been reported?
- Is the computer connected to a corporate network or resources?
- Is data stored to the corporate network or resources?
- Does anyone else use or have access to the computer?
- Is any data stored locally?

Potentially relevant data can be stored locally on a computer's storage media. The data can be broken down into several high-level categories, including documents, communication files, multimedia files, program files, system files, and archive files. Data can be in an active or deleted state. If deleted, data may be either recoverable or overwritten (non-recoverable).

The following are examples of these high-level categories of data and common file extensions associated with files within each category:

Documents (user-created or system created) – Microsoft DOCX, PPTX, XLSX files, and Adobe PDF files

Communication (Email container files) - Microsoft MSG, OLM, OST, PST files and HCL Notes / Lotus Notes NSF files

Multimedia (Photos, Videos, Audio files) - AVI, JPG, MOV, MP3, MP4, PNG, TIF

Program (Executable files) - BAT, COM, EXE

System (Files that allow a computer to function) - CAB, DLL, DRV, SYS

Archive (Files that are typically compressed and contain backup files) - 7ZIP, AR, GZ, ISO, RAR, TAR, TZ, ZIP

Now, with an understanding of the data categories, one can now focus on where the data resides on the computer. Often, user data is stored in a default location, or in a location designated by the IT Team. It may be necessary to interview Key Individuals, including a member of the IT Team to gather more information. Interviews are very helpful in better understanding how potentially relevant data may be organized. Although it is helpful to speak with the Key Individuals, it is more beneficial if, for example a Data Custodian can navigate to the locations on their local computer so that the full paths to the data can be documented. This process can be performed either in-person or remotely, via screen share. It is important that the data not be moved from the location in which it has been documented.

It is possible to store data in a variety of locations. So, if very little or no data is stored locally, where else could data reside? It is possible for data to reside within an email message on an email server or email archiving solution, on a network file share, within a corporate backup, with a cloud storage service, or on an external drive.

Here are some considerations when identifying if potentially relevant data is stored in these other locations.

Email Server / Email Archive

- Is the data embedded within or attached to an email message stored on an email server or within an email archive solution?

Network File Share

- Is the share accessible to the Data Custodian or others?

Corporate Backup Solution

- What gets backed up? How often? Where is the data stored? How long is the data stored?

External Storage Device

- Is the device corporate-issued / personally owned? Is the device available? Is usage of external storage devices allowed on computers?

Cloud Storage Service

- Is the data accessible to the Data Custodian or others?

Obtaining Access

There are several factors that may impact a data collection special-ist's ability to access the potentially relevant data on a local computer. It is common to encounter encryption solutions on computers, espe-cially on laptops which allow for mobility. It is important to identify if an encryption solution is present. If so, the name and version of the en-cryption solution should be documented. In a corporate environment, it is possible to encounter different versions of an encryption solution, and even different encryption solutions altogether. Gathering and docu-menting as much information as possible will help a data collection specialist plan accordingly. Depending on the type of encryption solu-tion, forensic tools may have native support; however, if not, different methodologies may need to be utilized to decrypt the data. The data collection specialist will need to work closely with the IT Team to pro-vide decryption keys or other information needed to decrypt the data. In some instances, it may be necessary to disable the encryption solu-tion or decrypt the data altogether for purposes of performing a data collection. It is also possible to encounter Basic Input Output System (BIOS) or boot passwords, when attempting to log on to a computer. In these scenarios, it will be necessary to obtain the password to allow the computer's boot process to continue, and the data on the local storage media to be accessible.

Data Collection Options

With the data on the computer's storage media now accessible, there are two data collection options that are available: a forensic image or a targeted collection. We have seen these terms before. A forensic image is also known as a "bitstream" image or "mirror" image. There are two types of forensic images, a physical image (applies to all areas of a storage media) or a logical image (applies to all areas of a storage volume). A targeted collection is defined as a forensic preservation or file copy of specific files or folders.

To fully understand the differences between a physical image and a logical image, it is important to dive in a bit further. A physical image is defined as a bit-by-bit copy of a storage media; it gets all, including files (active and deleted) and associated metadata on all storage volumes, unpartitioned areas of the storage media, Unallocated Space, File Slack and Partition Slack. A logical image, on the other hand, is a bit-by-bit copy of a storage volume; it includes files (active and deleted) and associated metadata, Unallocated Space and File Slack.

Let's take the types of forensic images to one more level. There are two types of physical or logical images: dead or live. A dead forensic image is recommended when a forensic investigation is required, as it provides a snapshot in time of the data stored on the storage media. A live forensic image is typically suitable for cases involving eDiscovery; there is some interaction with the computer's operating system and system files, and metadata is typically preserved for non-system files.

When a dead forensic image is performed, the source storage media is removed from the computer; therefore, the process is not dependent on the computer's hardware or software. A write blocker is utilized to prevent writes to the source storage media, and forensic software is utilized to generate a forensic image onto target storage media. The dead forensic image process does not leave any footprints on the computer or source storage media. Of course, when performing such a process, a data collection specialist needs to take precautions to protect the computer and source storage media, from static electricity, for example. Additionally, removing components from a computer's chassis may void some manufacturer's warranties.

When a live forensic image is performed, there is typically interaction between the computer's hardware and software. The process involves booting into the computer's operating system or a controlled environment and utilizing forensic acquisition software to generate a forensic image onto target storage media. If booting into the computer's operating system, the process will leave footprints. If booting into a controlled environment, it may recognize the source media as read-only; if read-only, the process will not leave footprints.

Of course, there are some things to consider when performing a live forensic image. The computer's BIOS / boot password will be needed, if enabled. Further, if encryption is enabled, it may be necessary to obtain decryption keys or information to decrypt the data stored on the

source storage media. As live forensic imaging typically requires interaction with the operating system, it may be necessary to obtain credentials (Data Custodian's or Administrator-level username and password)
to log into the operating system. The live forensic imaging process involves connecting target storage media to the computer; therefore, an
open port on the computer is required. This port must allow for writes
to external storage media. In some cases, it may be necessary for the
data collection specialist to work closely with the IT Team to relax any
security policies that may be set. More specifically, it may be necessary
to relax policies to allow the forensic image to be saved to the target
storage media and allow forensic acquisition / other software to be executed. It is recommended to have a member of the IT Team available
during the imaging process in case the data collection specialist requires any assistance. Last but certainly not least, because live imaging
requires powering on the computer, it is important that the power cord
for the computer is available, and the computer has sufficient battery
life for the data collection process to complete.

It is also possible to perform a targeted collection from a computer.
A targeted collection is defined as the forensic preservation or file copy
of specific files or folders. Targeted collections will include active files
only, and no File Slack. It is important to use tools and processes that
ensure files are copied in a manner that preserves their content and
metadata; this may require configuring a tool to run with specific options set.

The integrity of the forensic image or targeted collection is verified
utilizing a hash algorithm, such as MD5, SHA-1 or SHA-2.

There are pros and cons to forensic imaging and targeted collection.
Ultimately, a decision must be made, and it may be based on several
factors. If a forensic examination is required, a forensic image (more
specifically, a dead forensic image) is recommended, whereas if the
matter involves eDiscovery only, a targeted collection should suffice.
Remember that there can be a change in the scope of a matter. If only
specific files or folders are preserved and a re-collection is necessary
because of a change in scope or additional, potentially relevant data is
identified later, this can result in additional costs with individuals and
resources having to be available. Additionally, it may be possible that
data is no longer available or accessible due to the gap in time. Another

important consideration to be mindful of is that there may also be sensitivities involved, and the Key Individuals may want to exclude specific data from the data collection.

On average, it takes a data collection specialist 3-5 billable hours to perform a data collection of computer storage media. Several factors can impact the time involved, including the data collection method used, the storage capacity of the targeted media or volume of data, the speed of the Internet connection, and the speed of the hardware / software utilized.

A live forensic image / targeted collection can be performed on-site, in-lab or remotely.

A dead forensic image can only be performed on-site or in-lab, as it requires the data collection specialist to physically remove the source storage media from the computer's chassis.

Email

For over fifty years, email has allowed people to exchange messages between each other, using electronic devices. In 1965, email was first used at Massachusetts Institute of Technology (MIT); messages were stored on a central disk and users logged in remotely. The first usage of the @ symbol was in 1971 to exchange messages between systems. Today, over 300 billion emails are sent or received daily.

Protocols and Access

Email is sent and received via systems, programs, and protocols. An email server is a computer system located on premises, off premises, or in the cloud that sends and receives emails using standard protocols: Simple Mail Transfer Protocol (SMTP), Post Office Protocol (POP3) and Internet Message Access Protocol (IMAP). Email messages are stored within an email server mailbox. An email address (example: rob@robfried.com) identifies the email server mailbox to which email messages are delivered. An email client is a software program that accesses an email server and allows a user to send, receive, compose, and manage email messages.

Emails are sent and received thanks to protocols. SMTP is a sending protocol, which allows email messages to move across networks via Mail Transfer Agents (MTAs) to the proper email server and email mailbox. POP3 and IMAP are both receiving protocols. POP3 allows users to access and download email messages locally to a device. Once downloaded, email messages may be deleted from the email server. The POP3 protocol is ideal if only a single email client will access the email messages; otherwise, email messages can be sprinkled across multiple devices. IMAP allows users to access, organize and manipulate email messages on the email server. Messages do not have to be downloaded locally to a device. Multiple email clients can simultaneously access the email messages.

Identifying Relevant Data

Email server mailboxes can be accessed in a variety of ways. An email client can be utilized to access an email server mailbox or locally stored email, such as email container files or individual email files on a computer. An email app can be utilized to access an email server mailbox via a mobile device. An Internet web browser can be utilized to access an email server via a computer or mobile device.

Email can be stored in various locations. An email server stores email messages or related items within email mailboxes. A computer, network file shares, cloud storage services, and external media can all store email container files or individual email files. Many organizations also utilize email archiving solutions which preserves, and indexes email messages that are sent and received; they also allow email messages to be searched. Additionally, many organizations utilize backup solutions, including usage of backup media. This media can contain a backup of an email server, including database files, email container files or individual email files. Regarding mobile devices, email messages can be viewed via an app. Email messages can be downloaded locally but are typically stored on the email server.

Key Individuals should be interviewed to help identify all locations where relevant email messages are stored.

The following questions should be asked of the IT Team:

- Is there a Designated Administrator?
- What type of email server is in use? When was the email server implemented?
- Where is the email server located? On premises, off-premises, or is it cloud-based?
- When was the email server last updated?
- Has the email server ever been offline, for any reason?
- Was there a legacy email server? Were all the email messages

from the legacy email server migrated? If yes, when and was the process documented? Were all emails successfully migrated? Were any issues encountered during the process?

- Is there an email server mailbox storage quota?

- Is there a backup policy in place? If yes, what backup solution was utilized and how frequently? Where is the backup data stored?

- What email client(s) do Data Custodians utilize?

- Can Data Custodians store email container files locally, for offline use? If yes, is there a default or designated location where they are stored?

- Is there an email archiving solution in place? If yes, which solution and version? Is there a Designated Administrator?

The following questions should be asked of the IT Team / Legal Team:

- Is there an email retention policy in place (a list of parameters that define how long email messages should be kept for compliance or other business reasons)?

The following questions should be asked of the Data Custodian:

- How is the email server accessed? Via computer? Via mobile device?

- What email client / mobile app / website is used to access the email server?

- How are the email messages organized? Within mail subfolders?

- Are email folders named by individual, client, project, subject, etc.?

- Are read email messages saved or deleted regularly?

- Are email messages archived locally? Within an email container file? As individual email message files?

Based on the information learned, it may be necessary to perform data collections of email messages from multiple data sources that are identified. If necessary, email messages from multiple data sources can be de-duplicated.

Data Collection Options

There are several things to consider prior to performing any data collections. A Data Custodian can have multiple email mailboxes on an email server. An email mailbox may have been renamed; for example, if someone has gotten married and changed their surname. In many organizations, email aliases are utilized, so that emails are forwarded to a designated email mailbox. Additionally, Public Folders may be in use on an email server; this allows users to share content.

As with any data source, it is important to collect data in the most defensible and efficient manner. A data collection specialist must utilize tools and processes that ensure that messages and files are collected in a manner that preserves the contents of the messages, associated attachments (including those in the cloud), and metadata via forensic tools, an email server, an email client, or the tools or functionality available from an email service provider.

There are a variety of data collection types when it comes to email. Forensic tools can access email servers and email mailboxes. A data collection specialist will need information about the email server to connect to it. Account credentials will also need to be provided to the data collection specialist. Forensic tools often offer the ability to perform a targeted collection from email mailboxes, including exports based on date range and search term / keyword. Non-searchable text or images may be excluded. When dealing with an email server, a data collection specialist can perform either a full or targeted mailbox export. Whereas a full mailbox export provides an export of all email messages within an email server mailbox, a targeted mailbox export provides an export of specific items. A targeted mailbox export may include only individual email messages, email messages within a mail folder, email messages based on specific criteria: to / from an individual, to / from a domain name (i.e., @robfried.com), sent / received within a date range, and containing a search term / keyword (non-searchable text or images may be excluded). It is also possible to utilize email clients to access and export email messages. Email messages can be accessed or exported from a locally stored email container file or via live access to the email server. Email messages are typically exported to a newly generated email container file. Finally, email service providers offer tools and functionality to export or archive email messages from an email mailbox.

Data Collection Logistics and Considerations

Regardless of the data collection type performed, the data collection specialist will need to work closely with the Key Individuals. The IT Team or Designated Administrator can provide Administrator-level access to the email server mailbox or the email archive solution, with appropriate permissions to search and / or export email messages (for example: direct access to the email server, or web browser access to a cloud-based account). Additionally, the IT Team or Designated Administrator may be able to assist in decrypting email messages (if encryption is present). The Data Custodian can provide access to the device, or storage location of local email files, and identify the full path of the email files, account credentials to the email account, and verification codes (if enabled). It is important to note that if a Key Individual is sensitive about providing the password to their user account, it can be changed prior to the data collection.

One issue that often comes up is sensitivity around the collection of non-relevant data, and email is no exception. In these scenarios, a targeted collection can be performed. It is important to remember, however, that a re-collection of data may be necessary, if there is a change in the scope of the matter.

On average, it takes a data collection specialist 2-4 billable hours to perform a data collection of an email account. Several factors can impact the time involved, including the data collection method used, the volume of email messages, the speed of the computer / hardware being used to perform the data collection, whether the email service provider throttles data (limiting the amount of data that can be downloaded at a given time), the speed of the network / Internet connection, and the speed of the data source / email service provider storing the email to compile the search results, export the email messages, and make the email available for download.

Depending on the methodology used, data collections can be performed on-site, in-lab or remotely.

Network File Shares

Many corporate environments maintain network file shares to provide centralized file storage to users. There are several types of network devices utilized for storage, which are either a computer or computer appliance. Examples include a file server, a Network-Attached Storage (NAS) device or a Storage Area Network (SAN) device. A file server is a computer, configured as a server, running an operating system with tweaks for file sharing. A NAS device is a computer that is connected to a network and allows for data storage. A SAN device is a network of storage appliances.

It is important to discuss the differences between a NAS and SAN device. A NAS device provides shared storage over a shared network, utilizes a file system, and allows for easy management. A SAN device provides shared storage over a dedicated network, utilizes block storage and is fast but expensive. These devices may be located on-premises or off-premises and allow connected devices to access files and folders, freeing up storage space on local devices. The IT Team or Designated Administrator controls the security and maintenance of these devices, including managing permissions and backups.

There are different types of file shares, including a Home / User share and a Department / Group share. A Home / User share is a private location on a network storage device that is meant to be accessible only by an individual. It is common for the IT Team to store or backup the individual's data to this storage location. A Department / Group share is a storage location on a network storage device that is utilized by multiple individuals; typically, accessible only by specific individuals of a team or department. Often these shares are referred to by a name or mapped drive letter.

The IT Team may place limitations on the storage capacity of the network file shares, as they tend to be repositories for large volumes of data. It is important to consider what data to collect as collecting all the data may be burdensome. There may be significant time and costs involved in the data collection effort that should be discussed with the Key Individuals.

Depending on usage and saving habits of individuals, a network file share can be a very dynamic environment. Data may be frequently created, accessed, or modified. For convenience, frequently accessed network file shares may be mapped and assigned a persistent drive letter on a computer. The mapping is based on the Universal Naming Convention (UNC) path, which points to the specific location. An example of a UNC path: \\FileServer1\rfried\. This location may be mapped on a computer as drive letter: H.

Identifying Relevant Data

To identify where relevant data is stored on a file share, it may be necessary to interview the Key Individuals. Remember, network file shares can store a large volume of data. Files may be organized into folders. Additionally, files or folders may be named based on client, project subject, etc.

Data Collection Options

There are several data collection options to consider. There are two forensic image options that are available. A physical image generates a bit-by-bit copy of a storage device; it gets all, including files (active and deleted), and associated metadata on a storage device, unpartitioned areas, Unallocated Space, File Slack, and Partition Slack. A logical image generates a bit-by-bit copy of a storage volume, including files (active and deleted) and associated metadata, Unallocated Space, and File Slack.

It is important to use tools and processes that ensure files are copied in a manner that preserves their content and metadata; this may require configuring a tool to run with specific options set.

The integrity of the forensic image or targeted collection is verified utilizing a hash algorithm, such as MD5, SHA-1 or SHA-2.

Depending on policies, a backup of data from the network file share may exist. It is important to discuss the following with the IT Team:

- What type of backup exists?
- What storage media type and software were utilized for the backup?
- Are logs of the backup process available?
- Was metadata preserved during the backup process?
- How frequent are backups performed?
- When was the last backup performed?
- Where is the backup stored? On-premises / Off-premises? In the cloud?
- How accessible is the data?
- Can the backup be restored, if necessary?

Ultimately, a decision needs to regarding the data collection method to be utilized. To assist in this process, answer the following questions:

- Do you want to obtain a forensic image, targeted collection or utilize a backup?
- Is this an eDiscovery matter or a forensic investigation? If a forensic investigation, a forensic image may be necessary.
- What data will be available? Would any data be excluded? Are there sensitives regarding the data that need to be considered?
- Is all potentially relevant data identified? The Key Individuals may not recall the location of files or folders.

What if there is a change in scope for the matter? Will the key individuals be available to provide access to the data collection if a re-collection is necessary? Will the data still be accessible? What additional costs and time may be involved if a re-collection of data is necessary?

Data Collection Logistics and Considerations

There are several factors that should be considered when deciding on the data collection method to be utilized. The issue of business continuity is important; as a result, it may not be possible to power down a device to generate a forensic image. From a technical perspective, the device's storage media may be physically inaccessible. Additionally, the device's storage media may be configured as a Redundant Array of Independent Disks (RAID); technology that utilizes multiple storage media for data redundancy or improved performance. Remember, network file shares can store large volumes of data. The relevant data may only be a subset, and easily identified by the Key Individuals. The data collection specialist must utilize the most defensible and efficient methodology.

In most cases, a targeted collection of data from a network file share is sufficient. The integrity of the data, including associated metadata, will be preserved. A targeted collection eliminates the burden of collecting all. Additionally, a targeted collection can be performed by the data collection specialist, with the assistance of the IT Team; there is minimal involvement from the Data Custodians.

The data collection specialist needs a couple of pieces of information to perform a forensic preservation of data. It is important to obtain the UNC path, or if mapped, the drive letter of the targeted locations. Additionally, the data collection specialist will need access to a computer from which to perform the data collections. The computer must be configured with Administrator-level access to the targeted network file share locations, the ability to execute forensic tools, and an open port to attach target storage media with read / write permission.

On average, it takes a data collection specialist 2-4 billable hours to perform a data collection of a network file share. Several factors can impact the time involved, including the data collection method used, the storage volume of the targeted device or volume of data, the speed of the hardware / software being used to perform the data collection, and the speed of the network / Internet connection.

A live forensic image / targeted collection can be performed on-site, in-lab or remotely.

A dead forensic image can only be performed on-site or in-lab, as it requires the data collection specialist to physically remove the source media from the device.

Mobile Devices

Mobile devices such as smartphones, tablets or wearable devices are portable computing devices that fit in your hands. They have an operating system that allows the device to run applications and other programs. Most mobile device operating systems only work on specific hardware. For example, an Apple iPhone runs on iOS and a Google Pixel runs on Android.

Types of Data and Storage

Mobile devices are used for business and personal reasons, and data from these devices has become increasingly relevant as electronic evidence in litigation matters and investigations. There are two types of mobile devices: corporate-issued or personally owned. A corporate-issued mobile device is issued to eligible employees or contractors; it is owned or paid for by the corporation for the purpose of conducting business on behalf of the corporation. A personally owned mobile device is owned by an individual; it may be used to conduct business on behalf of a corporation. In recent years, many corporations have implemented Bring Your Own Device (BYOD) policies. These formal policies allow and specify how, personally owned devices may be used to conduct business on behalf of the corporation. Additionally, many corporations implement a Mobile Device Management (MDM) policy to secure, monitor and manage mobile devices.

Mobile devices can store a wide range of data, including communication (text messages / chats, email, voicemail), contacts, call logs, multimedia (photos / images, videos, audio, music), app data, documents, Internet browsing history, and location data. It is important to distinguish between text messages and chats. Text messages are electronic communications sent via a cellular network. There are two types of text messages: Short Message Service (SMS) and Multimedia Messaging Service (MMS); SMS contains text up to 160 characters per message and MMS contains multimedia. Chats are electronic communications that are sent via the Internet; they are also referred to as Over the Top (OTT) communications.

Mobile devices offer several storage types: internal, external and cloud. Internal storage is manufacturer-installed; an example is flash memory (a non-volatile memory chip that stores device and app data). External storage may or may not be present or utilized; examples include a memory card (small storage medium using flash memory that stores data, including photos and videos) or Subscriber Identity Module (SIM) card (small smart card / circuit board that enables communication between device and carrier, stores security data, and may contain SMS messages and contacts). Cloud storage may or may not be utilized; it may store device and app data.

What data types are relevant to the matter? It is important to consider the following questions:

- Was the mobile device in use during the relevant period? If no, was another mobile device in use? If yes, is the device or a backup accessible?

- What apps are installed or utilized? It may be necessary to interview the Key Individuals.

Data on mobile devices is dynamic; there is a constant exchange of data, as mobile devices can communicate with a cellular network, apps, servers, and connected devices. Mobile device data can be impacted by settings, time, power state, and the environment. It is important to identify any known limitations, as data may become inaccessible, and it may be necessary to perform a data collection as soon as possible.

The are several factors to consider when preparing a mobile device for a data collection. In terms of the device itself, the device will need to be powered on and operational, the passcode to unlock the device (if enabled) will need to be provided, a backup password (if utilized) will need to be provided, the device / app settings may need to be changed, MDM policies on the device (if present) will need to be relaxed (this will require assistance from the MDM Administrator), and the device may need to be connected to a computer. In terms of the device data, it is important to answer the following questions: Is the relevant data in a backup? stored on a computer? stored on external media? Stored with a cloud storage service?

Data Collection Options

The data collection specialist utilizes defensible and efficient methodologies and forensic tools to forensically preserve the local data on a mobile device. There are several data collection types that are available: physical acquisition, logical acquisition, file system acquisition, and manual acquisition. A physical acquisition utilizes a forensic tool to generate a bit-by-bit copy of the contents of the internal storage of a mobile device, including live and deleted data. A logical acquisition utilizes a forensic tool to copy live data for specific data types, including app data, call logs, text messages, images, photos, video, and audio. A file system acquisition utilizes a forensic tool to copy the live files within the mobile device's file system, including database files utilized by apps. It is important to note that the ability to recover deleted data types, such as text messages and chats, is dependent on the forensic tool's or forensic investigator's ability to parse such data, if it is still present, from the relevant database where it is stored. A manual acquisition involves navigating the various settings and apps on the mobile device, and documenting the contents of the screen via photograph, video, or transcription. This process may be very time consuming and only utilized when there is no alternate method available.

The data collection methodology utilized will be dependent on the forensic tool's support, the make / model of the mobile device, sensitivity regarding non-relevant data, and review requirements. Regarding the forensic tool's support, the data collection specialist must confirm the make / model of the device, operating system (and version) installed, and the app and version installed (especially important if data from a specific app is relevant). In terms of the make / model of the device, this is important as a physical acquisition is only available for specific makes / models. There is often sensitivity regarding the collection of non-relevant data. It may be necessary for the data collection specialist to develop customized workflows to identify and only collect relevant data. Regarding review requirements, data can be exported for review in a variety of formats, including native files. Additionally, it is possible to ingest data into a document review environment.

In terms of collecting relevant data that is not on a mobile device (SIM cards, external storage devices, and memory cards), the data collection specialist will utilize defensible methodologies and forensic tools to collect from these devices. Regarding cloud storage services, the data collection specialist will need account credentials (username / password) and any verification codes (if enabled) to be able to access the account and perform the data collection.

The number of mobile devices on the market today is constantly increasing. Additionally mobile device operating systems and apps are frequently updated. Do not forget, it's even possible for users to be beta testers of operating systems and apps, gaining access before the public. So it should come as no surprise that what a forensic tool supports today, it may not support tomorrow!

On average, it takes a data collection specialist 3-5 billable hours to perform a data collection of a mobile device. Several factors may impact this timing, including the data collection method used, the storage volume of the targeted device / media or volume of data, the speed of the Internet connection, and the speed of the hardware / software utilized.

Data collections of mobile devices can be performed on-site, in-lab or remotely.

Databases

A database is an organized collection of data. Databases may be vital to the operations of an organization, as key decisions are often made based on its content. Content may be updated at specific time intervals manually or in an automated manner.

Database Structure

To understand the structure of a database, there are several important terms to be aware of. Databases are comprised of tables, which store a group of related data, known as records. A field contains a single piece of data. Fields are organized into records. A field in a table that uniquely identifies a record is known as a primary key. To better understand the relationship between tables, a database map may be available. The content from tables can be combined to perform analysis and generate reports.

Information From Key Individuals

The Key Individuals should be interviewed as they may be able to provide information about the databases. Data Custodians and Business Stakeholders may be able to provide what specific databases are in use and the function and type of information that is available from each. Database Administrators may be able to provide responses to the following series of important questions:

- What type of databases are maintained? Example: Microsoft Access, Microsoft SQL, or Oracle.
- Is the database maintained on a server? Specific storage location?
- When was the database server implemented?

- Is the database server located on-premises or off-premises? In the cloud?

- How is data imported into the database? Manually, or in an automated manner?

- Are backups of the database generated? How often? Where are they stored? If stored off-site, are backups accessible? Can backups be restored, if necessary?

- Who has access to the database? Example: Business Stakeholders, Data Custodians, the Designated Administrator.

- What type of reports can be generated, and in what format? Example: A delimited text file.

- How are reports distributed? Example: Via email.

The Data Collection Process

Based on the scope of the matter, it is important to understand if it is sufficient to export only specific database records, or if a full export or backup of the database is needed. Additionally, the type of export needs to be considered; whether the exports can be provided in native file format, or if a specific format is required or has been requested.

There are several factors that a data collection specialist must consider when collecting from databases. The data collection specialist must ensure that they have Administrator-level access to the database. It is important to not only preserve data from the database but also any metadata; including data associated with database files, tables, records, and objects that may be relevant. Many organizations are sensitive to what data is included in data collections, and the data collection specialist may need to work closely with the Key Individuals to ensure that non-relevant data is excluded or redacted. Another factor that the data collection specialist needs to consider are any external files or objects; if there are any linkages to the database, the storage locations of these external files or objects will need to be identified.

The data collection specialist will need to work closely with the Key Individuals. Documentation is a key aspect of data collection involving databases. The data collection specialist will document information about the database server and the database itself, including documenting the relevant tables and relationships. Additionally, the data collection specialist will document steps taken (including screenshots, if possible), including queries that were compiled and executed. Exports and reports will be generated from the database and should have descriptive file names.

On average, it takes a data collection specialist 2-4 billable hours to perform a data collection of a database. There are several factors that may impact the timing of the data collection process, including the data collection method used, the size of the targeted database or volume of data, the speed of the network / Internet connection, and the speed of the hardware / software utilized.

Data collections of databases can be performed on-site, in-lab or remotely.

Cloud Storage

Billions of people utilize cloud storage services. A cloud storage service is a business that maintains and manages its customers' data and makes that data accessible over a network, usually the Internet. Data is stored beyond your four walls – it can be stored on servers around the world. Cloud storage offers many benefits including freeing up storage on local devices, sharing of large files, and accessing files from multiple devices.

Account Types

There are two different cloud storage account types: free and subscription based. Free accounts typically offer limited storage and features. Subscription-based accounts offer users additional storage, include advanced features for account management, and may include the ability to track user activity and file usage, and the potential to recover deleted data.

Accessibility and Synchronization

Data stored with cloud storage services can be uploaded, downloaded, organized, and accessed in several ways, including via an app, a software program, or a website. Many cloud storage services also allow users to synchronize their account data with multiple devices. It is important to understand where all relevant data resides and be aware that different versions of data may reside on different devices.

The Key Individuals may be able to provide additional information, and provide responses to the following:

- What cloud storage service(s) is / are being used?

- Is data commingled or organized? Is data organized by file name or folder name? It may be necessary to interview Key Individuals to identify relevant data. It may be necessary to conduct searches to identify relevant data (non-searchable text or images may be excluded).

- What is the anticipated storage volume of the data within the account?

- Will access be provided by the Data Custodian or IT Team? Account credentials will be needed (account password can be changed prior to the data collection). Verification codes will be needed (if enabled).

The Data Collection Process

Often, it is easy to upload data and difficult to export data, and the data collection specialist must ensure compatibility with the various forensic tools. Remember, the goal is to preserve data from cloud storage services forensically so that the integrity of the source data is maintained, including associated metadata. Alternative methodologies may need to be used, if necessary.

On average, it takes a data collection specialist 2-4 billable hours to perform a data collection of a cloud storage account. Several factors can impact the time involved, including the data collection method used, the volume of the data to be collected, the speed of the Internet connection, and whether the cloud storage service throttles data.

Data collections from cloud storage services can be performed on-site, in-lab or remotely.

Social Media

Billons of people use social media; interactive digitally mediated technologies that facilitate the creation or sharing of information, ideas, interests, and other forms of expression via virtual communities and networks. In recent years, there has been an increase in the number of requests to forensically preserve data from social media platforms. Social media often plays a role in many matters, including employment disputes, harassment, and personal injury.

Social media can play an important role in an investigation. For example, data from social media accounts can help establish a Data Custodian's activities and can verify critical events in a matter's timeline. To determine its relevance to the matter, it is important to consider the following:

- What social media platform(s) is / are being used?

- What specific content is relevant?

- Will private or public content be needed? Private content will require account credentials (account password can be changed prior to the data collection).

The Data Collection Process

Social media platforms are constantly evolving. It is important to forensically preserve data from social media accounts in a defensible and efficient manner. Forensic tools may be used to forensically preserve data (including associated metadata) from many social media platforms, including chats, posts, external links, and linked content. Many social media platforms have native tools that allow for the export of data too.

On average, it takes a data collection specialist 2-4 billable hours to perform a data collection of a social media account. Several factors can impact the time involved, including the data collection method used, the volume of data to be collected, the speed of the Internet connection, the speed of the hardware / software utilized, how long it takes a service provider to search the data or make it available for download, and whether the social media platform throttles data.

Data collections of social media accounts can be performed on-site, in-lab or remotely.

Remote Data Collections

Forensic preservation is a process that involves the handling and copying of electronic evidence, including its associated metadata, in such a manner that preserves its integrity. Any alteration may deem it inadmissible in a court of law. Regardless of where the data collection is performed, a data collection specialist will use methodologies that are defensible and efficient. Depending on the data source and several other factors, a remote data collection may be a viable option. A remote data collection is a series of defined procedures or processes, manual or automated, that are preconfigured by or under the direct guidance or supervision of a data collection specialist, who is not physically near the targeted data source.

Remote data collections have been developed and utilized for many years, for a wide array of data sources. In fact, depending on the data source, a remote data collection may be the preferred methodology. Note: A matter may have specific requirements or preferences that may require performing the data collection on-site or in-lab.

Qualifiers and Considerations

The option to perform a remote data collection is decided based upon several factors, including the scope of the project, the physical location and availability of the Data Custodian or device / media / data source, the distance, cost, and other logistics associated with traveling on-site and impeding deadlines.

The following are questions to think about when considering a remote data collection:

- Can the objectives defined within the scope of the matter be successfully achieved?

- Will all relevant data be accessible?

- Will the necessary parties be available to provide access to the device / media / data source?

- Is the Data Custodian tech-savvy to be able to assist, if necessary?

- Will the necessary information be provided to the data collection specialist to access the device / media or data source? (Account username, password, verification codes)

- Is there a stable, high-speed Internet connection available, if necessary, where the targeted device / media is located?

- Do estimated timelines associated with the remote data collections impact impeding deadlines?

It is also important to highlight that remote data collections require more interaction between the data collection specialist and the Data Custodian. The following is a typical workflow for a remote data collection:

1. The data collection specialist coordinates the shipment of a remote collection kit, which includes a Chain of Custody Form, encrypted target storage media with forensic tools, and a forensic computer with forensic tools (if required).

2. The data collection specialist schedules a teleconference or web meeting with the Data Custodian to perform the remote data collection.

3. The data collection specialist guides the Data Custodian through properly connecting / accessing the targeted device / media / data source.

4. The data collection specialist begins the data collection.

5. Upon completion of the data collection, the Data Custodian coordinates the shipment of the remote collection kit to the data collection specialist or a designated location.

Remote data collections are sufficient for eDiscovery matters. For matters where a forensic investigation may be required, it is recommended that a dead forensic image be generated, as not all areas of the source storage media may be forensically preserved during a remote data collection. Additionally, it may be necessary for the data collection specialist to interact with the source device's operating system, leaving footprints.

Remote data collections may use different methodologies and require more interaction with Data Custodians; however, the underlying foundation is the same as performing data collections on-site or in-lab - defensible and efficient methodologies are utilized.

Data Collection Considerations

Planning and Logistics

It is vital to properly plan for a data collection. The efficiency and success of the data collection will result from working closely with the various parties, including the Key Individuals. Some of the key questions to think about when planning for a data collection include:

- Are there any known deadlines?

- Are the Key Individuals identified and will they be available? Does anyone travel frequently? Are there any upcoming vacations scheduled that may impact the timing of a data collection?

- Are there multiple locations? Does anyone work remotely? Are there any upcoming meetings, where multiple Data Custodians may be in the same physical location?

- Will relevant data sources be available, accessible, and easily identifiable (including current / former / legacy data sources)?

- Is a secure work area available if the data collection specialist is required on-site? Can a schedule for data collections be developed? Will the data collection be conducted during or after business hours?

- Are there any laws or policies that may impact the data collection?

Data Source Considerations

Regarding the source device, the following questions should be considered:

- Is the Make, Model, Operating System, and version known?

- Do you know what programs or apps are installed?

- Do you know the version(s) of the targeted programs or apps?
- Do you know the storage capacity?
- Are usernames / passwords and passcodes available?
- Is encryption active? Is the encryption solution and version known? Is information or decryption keys available to decrypt the device / media / data?
- Can executable files be run? Can external storage media be attached and written to? Is a MDM policy in place (for mobile devices)?
- Are power cords / data cables available?

Regarding the source account, the following should be considered:

- Are usernames / passwords / verification codes (if enabled) available?

Additional considerations that should be on your radar include the following:

- Are any devices stored off-site, or is any data in the cloud?
- Are the devices or is the data immediately accessible? If not, what is required to access the devices or data, and when may the devices or data become available?

The location of the data collection depends on the methodology that the data collection specialist will utilize. An on-site data collection is an in-person data collection, performed by a data collection specialist at a designated or agreed upon location (examples: a place a business, a residence, or a public setting) and time. An in-lab data collection is a data collection performed by a data collection specialist at a forensic laboratory; the laboratory is equipped with specialized forensic hardware and software, is a secure, temperature-controlled environment, and protocols for evidence management exist. A remote data collection is a data collection performed by a data collection specialist who is not physically near the targeted data source; remote data collections can be performed using automated or guided processes.

The location of the data collection may also depend on the preference of the Key Individuals, the efficiency of the data collection methodology utilized and the overall project scope (other data sources may need to be collected and may be in the same or a different location), costs (including travel), the sensitivity of the collection, and the handling and transport of collected data.

The time to perform the data collection is dependent on several factors, including: the data collection method used, the storage volume of the targeted device / media or volume of data, the speed of the network / Internet connection, the speed of the hardware / software utilized, how long it takes a service provider to search the data or make it available for download, and whether the service provider throttles data.

Data Transfer

Once data is collected, it can be transferred in several ways, including, on-person or electronically. Regarding on-person transport, the data collection specialist or designated individual / service provider transports the data on encrypted target storage media to a designated location for storage or data processing; the designated individual / service provider may include a courier or multinational delivery service. Electronic transfer involves the data collection specialist or a designated individual uploading the data to a secure network location or site for storage or data processing; this typically involves use of a secure file sharing / transfer site or service. The preferred method of transport is based on several factors, including data volume, time sensitivity, and client preference (typically around data sensitivity and costs).

Cloud Storage Questionnaire

1. Does any relevant data exist on the service?
2. Is the account personally or company owned?
3. If utilized by the company, is there a Designated Administrator?
4. What type of account / subscription plan is active?
5. Is data comingled or organized?
6. Is data organized by file name or folder name?
7. What is the anticipated storage volume of the data within the account?
8. Will access (username / password) to the account be provided, if necessary?
9. Is multi-factor authentication enabled on the account?
10. Do you use a personal cloud storage service account to conduct company business?

Computers Questionnaire

1. What is the make / model of your computer?

2. Is the computer company or personally owned?

3. When was the computer issued?

4. Was the computer in use during the relevant period?

5. Was the computer new or repurposed when issued?

6. Was the computer issued as part of a technology refresh? If yes, was the data migrated over from a previous computer? If not migrated, is the previous computer or its data accessible?

7. Have any issues with the computer been reported? Specify any known dates.

8. Does anyone else use or have access to the computer? List names.

9. Is the computer connected to a corporate network or resource?

10. Is any data stored locally? If yes, where is relevant data stored?

11. How is potentially relevant data organized?

12. Do you use any external storage devices?

13. Is the external storage device a company or personally owned?

14. Is the external storage device available?

15. Is the usage of external storage devices on computers allowed?

16. Is there any encryption solution being used on the computer? If yes, what is the encryption solution and version installed? Is the decryption information available?

17. Is a BIOS / boot password required to log onto the computer?

18. Is the local data backed up to another location? External media? Network file share? Cloud storage service?

19. Is there a corporate backup solution in use? If yes, what gets backed up and how often? Who has access to the backups? Where is the data saved? How long is the data saved for?

20. Do you use any computers at home to conduct company business?

Databases Questionnaire

1. What types of databases are used and maintained?
2. What is the function of each database? What information is available?
3. Is the database stored on a database server? If not, where is it stored?
4. When was the database server implemented?
5. Is the database server located on-premises or off-premises? In the cloud?
6. Is there a designated database Administrator?
7. How is data imported into the database?
8. Is the database backed up? If yes, what types of backups are generated? How often?
9. Where are the database backups stored? Can they be restored, if necessary?
10. Who has access to the database?
11. What types of exports / reports can be generated? What format?
12. Where are files or objects associated with the database stored?
13. How are the reports distributed?

Email Questionnaire

1. What type of email server is in use?

2. Is there a designated email Administrator?

3. Is the email server located on-premises or off-premises, or is it cloud-based?

4. When was the email server implemented?

5. Was there a legacy email server? If yes, were all emails from the legacy email server migrated? If yes, when and was the process documented? If yes, were any issues encountered during the process?

6. When was the email server last updated?

7. Has the email server ever been offline, for any reason?

8. Is there an email server mailbox storage quota?

9. Is there a backup policy in place? If yes, what backup solution is used and how often? Where is the backup data stored?

10. Is there an email retention policy in place?

11. What email client(s) or website(s) is / are used to access the email server mailbox?

12. What is the specific email address, including domain? (Example: rob@robfried.com)

13. Are any email messages encrypted? Can the necessary information be provided to decrypt the email messages?

14. Are email messages organized? If yes, within mail subfolders?

15. Are folders named by individual, client, project, subject?

16. Are read email messages saved or deleted regularly?

17. Are email messages archived locally? Saved within an email container file? Saved as individual email messages? Is there a specific location where they are stored?

18. Is there an email archiving solution in place? If yes, which product and version?

19. Do you use any personal email addresses to conduct company business? If yes, please provide the specific email addresses, including domain (for example: rob@robfried.com)?

Mobile Devices Questionnaire

1. What is the make / model of your mobile device?

2. What operating system, and version are in use?

3. Is the mobile device personally owned or company issued? If company issued, is there a designated Administrator?

4. Was the mobile device in use during the relevant period?

5. If not, was another mobile device in use?

6. Is the device or a backup of the data on the device accessible?

7. Do you store documents locally on the device?

8. Do you engage in substantive communications that may be relevant to the matter on the mobile device?

9. What apps are installed or utilized? What version?

10. Do you back up your device? Locally or in the cloud?

11. If yes, when was the last time a backup was performed? Is the backup password protected? If yes, would you be able to provide the password?

12. Is a passcode enabled on the device? If yes, would you be able to provide the passcode?

13. Is there a Mobile Device Management (MDM) solution enabled? Is there a designated MDM Administrator?

14. Do you use a personal mobile device to conduct company business?

Network File Shares Questionnaire

1. What type of device is the Network File Share (File Server, NAS, SAN)?

2. Is there a Designated Administrator?

3. Do you have a Home / User share? If yes, do you store documents there? Is it a mapped drive? Is it referred to by a specific name?

4. Are files organized into folders? Are files or folders named based on client, project, subject?

5. What type of backup exists? Was a specific solution or process utilized for the backup?

6. How frequent are the backups performed?

7. When was the last backup performed?

8. Was metadata of the data preserved during the backup process?

9. What storage media type and software were used for the backup?

10. Are logs of the backup process available?

11. Where is the backup stored? On-premises? Off-premises? In the cloud?

12. How accessible is the data?

13. Can the backup be restored, if necessary?

Social Media Questionnaire

1. What specific social media platform(s) do you use?
2. Does any relevant data exist on the platform? For example: posts, communication, documents?
3. Is the account personally or company owned?
4. If utilized by the company, is there a Designated Administrator?
5. Will access (username / password) to the account be provided, if necessary?
6. Is multi-factor authentication enabled on the account?

Knowledge Assessment

Electronically Stored Information (ESI)

1. ESI is fragile.
   True or False

2. A Chain of Custody Form includes all the following information except:
   a. Matter name
   b. Evidence number assigned
   c. The password to the device
   d. The date / time a device was transferred
   e. The make / model of a device

3. A new Chain of Custody Form must be completed each time there is a transfer of possession for a device.
   True or False

4. Which of the following is included in a forensic image?
   a. Active files
   b. Deleted files
   c. File Slack
   d. Unallocated Space
   e. All the above

5. Which of the following is a hash algorithm that is used to generate a digital fingerprint of the contents within a file?
   a. SHA-4
   b. MD4
   c. MD5
   d. None of the above

Computers

6. SSD is the acronym for Stable State Drive.
   True or False

7. Which of the following file extensions is not an executable file?
   a. .EXE
   b. .BAT
   c. .DLL
   d. .COM

8. A dead forensic image is recommended for a forensic investigation.
   True or False

9. A Data Custodian may backup data from their computer to which of the following locations?
   a. Network file share
   b. External hard drive
   c. Cloud storage service
   d. All the above

10. Which of the following file extensions is associated with a communication file?
    a. .ZIP
    b. .NSF
    c. .AR
    d. .TIF

Email

11. Which of the following is a protocol associated with sending email?
    a. SMTP
    b. IMAP
    c. POP3
    d. None of the above

12. A Data Custodian can only have one (1) mailbox on an email server.
    True or False

13. With an IMAP email account, a user can organize messages on the email server.
    True or False

14. Which of the following is not a function of an email client?
    a. Allows a user to access their messages in their mailbox
    b. Allows a user to send email messages
    c. Allows a user to receive email messages
    d. Allows a user to delete a mailbox on the server
    e. Allows a user to compose an email message

15. Email can be stored in which of the following locations?
    a. Cloud
    b. Local device
    c. Backup media
    d. Email archiver
    e. All the above

Network File Shares

16. A Home Share may be used by the IT Team to store a backup of a Data Custodian's computer data.
True or False

17. The acronym UNC stands for which of the following:
    a. Universal Network Computer
    b. Universal Node Convention
    c. Universal Naming Convention
    d. United Naming Convention

18. Which of the following devices does not allow for network storage?
    a. UNC
    b. SAN
    c. NAS
    d. File Server

19. It is always recommended to power down a network file server to generate a forensic image.
True or False

20. A data collection specialist will typically require a workstation configured with the following, except:
    a. Administrator-level access to the targeted folders and files
    b. Ability to run forensic tools
    c. An open HDMI port to connect an external hard drive
    d. An open USB port to connect an external hard drive

Mobile Devices

21. Which of the following is not a type of mobile device?
    a. Laptop
    b. Smartphone
    c. Tablet
    d. Desktop
    e. Watch

22. The acronym MDM stands for which of the following?
    a. Mobile Device Manufacturer
    b. Mobile Device Management
    c. Mobile Device Model
    d. Mobile Device Module
    e. None of the above

23. A BYOD policy allows an employee to use a personally owned device to conduct business on behalf of the corporation.
    True or False

24. SMS messages allow up to how many characters per message?
    a. 175
    b. 160
    c. 150
    d. 125

25. A SIM card cannot contain SMS messages.
    True or False

Databases

26. A table stores records.
    True or False

27. Which of the following is a type of database?
    a. Oracle
    b. SQL
    c. SQLite
    d. Access
    e. All the above

28. Fields are organized into tables.
    True or False

29. A field contains a single piece of information.
    True or False

30. A Primary Key is a field in a table that uniquely identifies a record.
    True or False

Cloud Storage

31. Which of the following is not a benefit of cloud-based storage services?
    a. Frees up local storage
    b. Allows for sharing of files
    c. Always offers unlimited storage
    d. Allows access from multiple devices

32. A data collection specialist only needs a Data Custodian's password to access their cloud storage account.
    True or False

33. Free cloud storage accounts typically offer unlimited storage.
    True or False

34. Paid cloud storage accounts typically offer which of the following benefits?
    a. Potential to recover deleted data
    b. Logging of user activities
    c. Additional storage
    d. Advanced features related to account management
    e. All the above

35. All cloud storage accounts can be collected using forensic tools.
    True or False

Social Media

36. Private content from social media accounts will require a Data Custodian's user credentials.
    True or False

37. Forensic tools are the only way to export data from social media platforms.
    True or False

38. Social Media data can assist in investigating a timeline of events that may be relevant to a matter.
    True or False

39. Forensic tools can collect public and private data without the need for a Data Custodian's credentials.
    True or False

40. Which of the following types of social media content can be collected using a forensic tool?
    a. Posts
    b. Chats
    c. External links
    d. Linked content
    e. Metadata
    f. All the above

Remote Data Collections

41. Whenever possible, cloud data collections should be performed on-site.
True or False

42. Which of the following is a qualifier for performing a remote collection?
a. Impending deadlines
b. The scope of the project
c. The location of the source device
d. All the above

43. The tech-savviness of the Data Custodian is important when considering whether a remote data collection should be an option.
True or False

44. A forensic computer is always included with a remote collection kit.
True or False

45. A remote collection typically requires more interaction with a Data Custodian.
True or False

Data Collection Considerations

46. Which of the following is an advantage of an in-lab data collection?
    a. Temperature-controlled environment
    b. Protocols for evidence management
    c. Availability of forensic hardware and software
    d. Enhanced security
    e. All the above

47. The amount of data collected does not impact the method by which data is transferred.
    True or False

48. Which of the following is not needed by a data collection specialist to access a cloud storage account?
    a. The password
    b. The 2-Factor Authentication code
    c. The username
    d. The date the account was created

49. Data throttling can impact the time associated with a data collection.
    True or False

50. Which of the following is not necessarily important to know, when preparing for a data collection involving a mobile device?
    a. The Make / Model
    b. The installed version of the operating system
    c. The Name associated with the device
    d. The installed version of the targeted app

References

Boor, D., Jaco, J., Gumz, E., Horrigan, D. and Fried, R., 2021. Social Media Considerations and Challenges in eDiscovery. *Peer to Peer: ILTA's Quarterly Magazine*, (Fall 2018), pp.58-69.

EDRM | Empowering the Global Leaders of eDiscovery. 2021. EDRM Model | EDRM. [online] Available at: <https://edrm.net/edrm-model/>.

Fried, R., 2022. Be That Trusted Advisor. Forensic Focus, Available at: <https://www.forensicfocus.com/articles/be-that-trusted-advisor/>.

Fried, R., 2021. B.Y.O.D. Policies: When a Personally Owned Device Contains Potentially Relevant Data. *Professional Investigator Magazine*, (175), pp.13-15.

Fried, R., 2020. Cloud Storage Services: ESI Beyond But Within Your Reach. [Blog] *Legaltech news*, Available at: <https://www.law.com/legaltechnews/2020/07/09/cloud-storage-services-esi-beyond-but-within-your-reach/>.

Fried, R., 2021. Forensic Preservation and Examination of Digital-Based Evidence During a Pandemic. *Professional Investigator Magazine*, (172), pp.14-15.

Fried, R., 2021. It is not enough to know. You also need to educate and communicate. *The Legal Investigator*, (2021 Spring Edition), pp.12-13.

Fried, R. and Gungor, A., 2021. Email Evidence: Be Careful How You Click. *Professional Investigator Magazine,* (178), pp. 56, 58.

Fried, R. and Lee, H., 2021. Applying Forensic Fundamentals to the Evolving Evidence of Today. *Professional Investigator Magazine*, (177), pp.58-60.

Fried, R. and Piernot, D., 2021. I say "Alexa" and you say "Franziska." *Professional Investigator Magazine*, (176), p.60.

Fried, R. and Muzzin, Z., 2022. Cloud Attachments: Inside an Email – Yet Stored Outside. Professional Investigator Magazine, (179), pp. 56-57.

About the Author

Robert B. Fried is a seasoned expert and industry thought-leader, with over twenty years of experience performing data collections and forensic investigations of electronic evidence. He is the Senior Vice President and Global Head of Sandline Global's Forensics and Investigations practice. In this role, Robert leads the day-to-day operations of the practice, overseeing the forensic services offered to the firm's clients, including data collections, forensic analysis, expert testimony, and forensic consultation.

Prior to joining Sandline Global, Robert held senior-level positions within the digital forensic practices at global professional services firms. Additionally, Robert was a Computer Crime Specialist at the National White Collar Crime Center (NW3C), where he developed and instructed computer forensic and investigative training courses for federal, state, and local law enforcement agencies.

Robert attained a BS and MS in Forensic Science, and certificates in Law Enforcement Science, Computer Forensic Investigation, and Information Protection and Security from the University of New Haven. Robert serves on the Board of Advisors for the Masters in Investigations program at the University of New Haven.

Robert holds and actively maintains the following industry certifications: Access Data Certified Examiner (ACE), Certified Forensic Computer Examiner (CFCE), EnCase Certified Examiner (EnCE), GIAC Certified Forensics Analyst (GCFA), Chainalysis Cryptocurrency Fundamentals Certification (CCFC), Chainalysis Reactor Certification (CRC), and C4 Certified Bitcoin Professional (CBP). Robert is a licensed Professional Investigator in Michigan and is a licensed Private Investigator in New York. Robert has been appointed a Special Master and has provided oral and written expert testimony on behalf of his clients.

Robert serves on the EC-Council Global Advisory Board for the Computer Hacking Forensic Investigator (CHFI) certification. He is an active member of professional organizations, including: American Academy for Professional Law Enforcement (AAPLE), American Academy of Forensic Sciences (AAFS), Associated

Licensed Detectives of New York State (ALDONYS), Fraternal Order of Investigators (FOI), High Technology Crime Investigation Association (HTCIA), International Association for Identification (IAI), International Association of Computer Investigative Specialists (IACIS), National Association of Legal Investigators (NALI), National Council of Investigation & Security Services (NCISS), New York Academy of Public Education (NYAPE), New York Metro InfraGard Members Alliance (NYM-IMA), Society of Professional Investigators (SPI), Women's Bar Association of the District of Columbia (WBA), and World Association of Detectives, Inc. (WAD).

Often sought after for his exceptional ability to convey forensics related topics, Robert is a frequent speaker at industry events. Robert has been a guest on industry podcasts and has been published in several professional publications, including: Legaltech news, NALI's The Legal Investigator (recipient of The Anthony Golec Editor / Publisher Award in June 2021), and the International Legal Technology Association's (ILTA) Peer to Peer Magazine. Robert is the author of PI Magazine's CyberSleuthing Department, where he shares insightful content on topics relating to digital forensics, eDiscovery, data privacy, and cybersecurity.

Knowledge Assessment Answer Key

Electronically Stored Information (ESI)

1. ESI is fragile.
   True or False

2. A Chain of Custody Form includes all the following information except:
   c. The password to the device

3. A new Chain of Custody Form must be completed each time there is a transfer of possession for a device.
   False

4. Which of the following is included in a forensic image?
   e. All the above

5. Which of the following is a hash algorithm that is used to generate a digital fingerprint of the contents within a file?
   c. MD5

Computers

6. SSD is the acronym for Stable State Drive.
   False

7. Which of the following file extensions is not an executable file?
   c. .DLL

8. A dead forensic image is recommended for a forensic investigation.
   True

9. A Data Custodian may backup data from their computer to which of the following locations?
   d. All the above

10. Which of the following file extensions is associated with a communication file?
    b. .NSF

Email

11. Which of the following is a protocol associated with sending email?
    a. SMTP

12. A Data Custodian can only have one (1) mailbox on an email server.
    False

13. With an IMAP email account, a user can organize messages on the email server.
    True

14. Which of the following is not a function of an email client?
    d. Allows a user to delete a mailbox on the server

15. Email can be stored in which of the following locations?
    e. All the above

Network File Shares

16. A Home Share may be used by the IT Team to store a backup of a Data Custodian's computer data.
    True

17. The acronym UNC stands for which of the following:
    c. Universal Naming Convention

18. Which of the following devices does not allow for network storage?
    a. UNC

19. It is always recommended to power down a network file server to generate a forensic image.
    False

20. A data collection specialist will typically require a workstation configured with the following, except:
c. An open HDMI port to connect an external hard drive

Mobile Devices

21. Which of the following is not a type of mobile device?
d. Desktop

22. The acronym MDM stands for which of the following?
b. Mobile Device Management

23. A BYOD policy allows an employee to use a personally owned device to conduct business on behalf of the corporation.
True or False

24. SMS messages allow up to how many characters per message?
b. 160

25. A SIM card cannot contain SMS messages.
False

Databases

26. A table stores records.
True

27. Which of the following is a type of database?
e. All the above

28. Fields are organized into tables.
False

29. A field contains a single piece of information.
True

30. A Primary Key is a field in a table that uniquely identifies a record.
True

Cloud Storage

31. Which of the following is not a benefit of cloud-based storage services?
c. Always offers unlimited storage

32. A data collection specialist only needs a Data Custodian's password to access their cloud storage account.
False

33. Free cloud storage accounts typically offer unlimited storage.
False

34. Paid cloud storage accounts typically offer which of the following benefits?
e. All the above

35. All cloud storage accounts can be collected using forensic tools.
False

Social Media

36. Private content from social media accounts will require a Data Custodian's user credentials.
True

37. Forensic tools are the only way to export data from social media platforms.
False

38. Social Media data can assist in investigating a timeline of events that may be relevant to a matter.
True

39. Forensic tools can collect public and private data without the need for a Data Custodian's credentials.
False

40. Which of the following types of social media content can be collected using a forensic tool?
f. All the above

Remote Data Collections

41. Whenever possible, cloud data collections should be performed on-site.
False

42. Which of the following is a qualifier for performing a remote collection?
d. All of the above

43. The tech-savviness of the Data Custodian is important when considering whether a remote collection should be an option.
True

44. A forensic computer is always included with a remote collection kit.
False

45. A remote collection typically requires more interaction with a Data Custodian.
True

Data Collection Considerations

46. Which of the following is an advantage of an in-lab data collection?
e. All the above

47. The amount of data collected does not impact the method by which data is transferred.
False

48. Which of the following is not needed by a data collection specialist to access a cloud storage account?
   d. The date the account was created

49. Data throttling can impact the time associated with a data collection.
   True

50. Which of the following is not necessarily important to know, when preparing for a data collection involving a mobile device?
   c. The Name associated with the device

Index